A Nap in Bed

By Cameron Macintosh

I am on my bed to nap.

Jan has her jet.

I get on the bed to nap.

My dog Ben gets his hen.

Tap, tap, tap!

I am on my bed to nap.

Dom has his red top.

Hop, hop, hop!

Jan, Ben and Dom
go on the rug.

I go on the rug, too.

I can nap!

CHECKING FOR MEANING

1. What toy did the dog play with? *(Literal)*

2. Who is on the rug at the end of the story? *(Literal)*

3. Why couldn't the girl go to sleep on her bed? *(Inferential)*

EXTENDING VOCABULARY

top	What is a *top*? What are the sounds in this word? What is another meaning for the word *top*?
hop	Read the word *hop*. What does it mean? What are other words you know that describe the way you or your toys move? E.g. skip, slide, roll.
rug	What is a *rug*? What is another word that means the same as *rug*? What sounds are in that word?

MOVING BEYOND THE TEXT

1. Why do you sometimes need a nap during the day?

2. What are some toys you own that make a noise when you play with them?

3. What are some quiet activities you can do inside?

4. Which pets sometimes sleep inside the house? Why?

SPEED SOUNDS

Dd	Jj	Oo	Gg	Uu

Cc	Bb	Rr	Ee	Ff	Hh	Nn

Mm	Ss	Aa	Pp	Ii	Tt

PRACTICE WORDS

on

bed

jet

run

Run

not

get

Get

dog

gets

top

Dom

Hop

rug

hop

red

Jan

and